MW01103826

Night Water Reflections

JOHN V. LAMOTTE, JR.

authorHOUSE®

AuthorHouse™
1663 Liberty Drive
Bloomington, IN 47403
www.authorhouse.com
Phone: 1-800-839-8640

First published by AuthorHouse   8/31/2010

ISBN: 978-1-4520-6726-1 (sc)
ISBN: 978-1-4520-6727-8 (e)

Library of Congress Control Number: 2010912576

Printed in the United States of America

This book is printed on acid-free paper.

Contents

Foreword   ix

Poetry   xi

Arson Blaze   1

Meteorology   3

The Assembly Life   5

Night Water Reflections   7

Nuclear Winter   9

Migratory Birds   11

Scorched Heart Policy   12

New York City Street Vendor   14

Spring Start   16

A Birthday in East L.A.   17

November Woods   19

A Wedding Blessing   20

Empty Winter Trackage   23

The Waitress is a Witness   25

Growth Cycles   30

Wind Listening   32

A Birthday Card for Pat-Heart   34

Buffalo Grass   36

August Tundra Hell   38

Binding Questions with Know Answers   40

Hate & Hope   43

Month of Sundays   45

Moon Talk on a Daily Basis   46

The Warden   51

Candled Opera   53

Dream Deprivation   55

Lonely Winter Love Letter   56

Momentary J. Man   58

Grandma's Nightmares   59

House & Garden Beautiful   62

Graffiti Gods   64

Coldwater Woman   67

Border Wars   68

Landmark Status   70

Pre-Storm Warning   73

Eulogy for the Good Witch   75

Hem House   77

Pardon Me, A Prisoner's Plea   79

Harvest Heart   81

Ice Station Chicago   82

Social Worker Burnout   84

Stay Tuned   87

Middle America   88

Oak Log Fires   90

In Remission ???   91

Patience   93

Paris Eyes   95

Stillbirth   97

Catherine Cathedral   99

Night Blanket   101

Lake Powell, Utah   103

Summer Start   105

Macho Marriage, Inc.   106

Chicago Highway Approach   108

Ash Pit Skies   110

The Shopster   111

Shadow Lands   114

Indigo Lies   118

Bold Birds   120

The Sow's Purse   121

Industrial Romance   122

The Carpet Remnant   124

Rocket Men – Wonder Women   127

Sky Painter   129

The Drug Czars   131

A Prairie Sermon   135

Lake Arrowhead, California   137

Poetry   138

About The Author   141

FOREWORD

Night Water Reflections is a collection of poetry that I have written over the course of my life from those halcyon high school days until today. This daily passion play has been scripted in and out of my mind on scraps of paper, notepads and napkins... and on any other carbonless cord cut, thin sliced wood sheaths I could find at my moments of love, anger, joy or sorrow... aggravation, exaltation or creative inspiration. These poetry pieces were often crafted late at night when I should have been sleeping and couldn't shut down my mind or when I should have been paying more attention to the road when driving or in odd places like country barns or city alleys.

My interest in creative writing was nurtured and influenced early on by my mother Paula, my family's iron butterfly, my grandmothers Anna and Edith, our resident philosophers, and my father John's profession of social work. This writing interest was also later driven by my chosen profession of city planning and my love of cities... small or large, great and strong, struggling or declining or a combination thereof... and especially "my kinda town"... Chicago, the city of big shoulders, big hearts, political circuses, "wait 'till next year" sports and great, down-to-earth Middle American people.

This poetry "thing" was also inspired by the poets and writers I discovered throughout the years, whose works I found laying around classrooms and backrooms, and hiding there amongst the colorful paper cocoons set under so many Christmas trees by Santa Claus, Mom and Dad.

I remember how my mother would ask me to write stories about anything and everything in gallant attempts to keep an active young boy from mischief whenever I had an idle minute or hour, and nothing to do. Over the years, she has continued to fill my heart and my library with beautiful words and books.

My parents must have realized that there was something poetic going on when their All-American boy from Illinois wrote a Halloween horror story assignment for a freshman English class about a duck hunt, but told it from the ducks perspective!!! This dark, chilling October story coming after discovering the wonderful world of girls and gushy love notes in junior high school.

It was in high school that I also came across a quote that became forever etched in my mind... *"Ideas are born in the minds of people, but are brought into being at the point of a pencil"*. From that moment on, I usually had some sort of writing instrument and paper product nearby so I could capture the ideas and thoughts that race continually through my mind, whether they were real feelings or make believe word crafting.

I was also inspired by Betty Southard, my high school English teacher, who positively reinforced my interest in creative writing, even when she knew I wasn't paying attention to her grammar drills and sentence diagramming lessons.

Night Water Reflections is dedicated to my family, past and present... the grand grandmas, parents...John Sr. and Paula, sisters...Patti and Marla, brothers-in-law...Joe and Tom, nephews...Mike, Chris, Johnny, Colin, Danny and Alex...the LaMottes, Mahers, Keenans and Henris... and my fiancé Jennifer....and my friends... for without them there would be no me. For it is they from whom I derive my content and my interest in life's interesting turns. For they, like cities and never ending prairies, spark my imagination and stir my soul...

POETRY

Poetry is a bunch of thoughts and ideas… passions and angry moments… some joy juice, a little laughter and non-finite or quick feelings… lying in ink on paper in a book. Poetry can be like peering into everyday dreams or like ripping open invisible wounds or just a bunch of random mindless thoughts and shards of silly or very serious stuff.

Poetry allows you to create sound bites that are not political or can be or bite sounds that may make sense to everyone but reporters and spin-doctors. Poetry allows people to be free form, creative creatures that can ride rough shod over the lucid language of a society once hell-bent on perfect phrases, pauses and clauses, with no dangling participles.

Poetry allows one to be completely free in expression like an artist… but most importantly it captures our thoughts, feelings, moods and experiences in a different, possibly even complex way that can be easily opened for all to see… like a one way, non-refundable ticket down Robert Frost's famous "path not taken"… virtual journeys whenever, wherever we want to travel.

Poetry is a license to drive on the wrong side of the language road we must travel each day and a "license to thrill". It can be fun and games… it can be mind games… it can be the deep exploring of heart and soul mines.

When reading this book, this poetry, I ask that you think not of this book itself or its paper or its ink or the sentences or the individual words. But think of what the words and sentences say, and may mean as they lay together in ink, on paper, in a book.

John LaMotte

ARSON BLAZE

In a big, big city...
on a mean mayoral street,
where trash hovers above
broken curb and gutter,
where garbage overflows
dented aldermanic signature cans,
where too many people live
in decayed housing,
there is a man with glazed eyes,
a gasolined rag,
and a match in his hands...

A spark, then a flame,
ignites the rag, the trash
and then the housing.

Flames grow
and quickly spread,
up and through
a rotten apartment building,
licking every wall,
seeking every corner.

The flames are faster
than an old man
and he is engulfed,
as is a wailing baby
who is just as helpless.

Smoke fills up a room
and fills up the lungs
of a sleeping boy
who does not awaken.

Sirens scream
and red lights flash,
as rumbling fire engines
race down narrow streets
toward the wild, raging flames.

A crowd gathers,
water sprays, axes crash
and a mother calls hysterically
for a baby who is helpless
and a boy who is sleeping.

Voices cry out from within,
as smoke billows bold
through broken windows,
then brilliant flames
flash giant and stark
against the dark, dirty building
and the night...
and there are cries no more.

Sweaty, coughing firefighters
with charcoal tinged faces,
carry out a lifeless body,
then another... and another.

A man with haunting eyes
standing silent in the gathering crowd,
has hands that smell of gasoline.

METEOROLOGY

The heavens...
and earth reactions.
The respiratory condition
of a sky head
in constant nasal flux.

Dry and irritated
desert dust bowls,
in lush urban grow gardens.

Wet and wild explosive theory,
ringing from cumulus
and even nimbus,
through the daily weather towns.

Lightning flashes,
like distant incendiary bombs
or sudden white slashes
on old dark movie reel nights.

What do they mean the sky sparks ???

The outlook, a report,
a thunder retort,
filling fields with rain
and hearts with hope.

The watcher, a formulator,
of weathered opinions
on the scattershot behavior
and biological discharge
of fleeting, sheeting motor clouds
so hard to catch, count or classify.

Sunny and clear,
with occasional slashing sleet
and periodic intermittent
sprinkle showers, thick fogs
and very low visibility.

Drive carefully,
but forget your hat
and your green umbrella,
stay home,
enjoy the storm sequence,
and sled up
the snow crested rain hills.

THE ASSEMBLY LIFE

The bodies of some
and their internalized souls,
go on and on
fatigued, faded
and maybe desperate,
in a quiet machine-like way,
day in and day out,
punch in and punch out
hour after hour
minute by minute
of taking it, just making it
to the factory whistle goal.

Dawn.... again,
in the automatic cycle
of rise and exist,
continually at the edge
of cease and desist.

The bodies of some,
stumbling and sputtering
often mind numb,
through the daily mileage
of taking it and it,
taking its toll,
until the gears and cogs
finally lock up, freeze and say no,
as numbness and
a mere, sheer existence
that went on for so long
no longer goes on,
and on that day
the walking wounded wreckage stops...

while silent buses
pointed toward fast factories,
start again, out there
in the cold dark air
of the early morning bus barn.

NIGHT WATER REFLECTIONS

Night and night time...
With the right tone
can be any time
any place,
even anywhere.

Night
and the water below
can be restful and peaceful,
or beautiful, bodacious
and star shine sparkling
with so many bright lights
silhouetted black/white
on tall buildings,
seawalls and lovers lives.

And yet,
night can be a fright
and bad
and sad to some,
when they let it,
if they let it...
when the water below
mirror mimes reflections
that can appear tough,
tenacious and even cruel.

The water below the night
let it reflect tight,
and ripple right
the good times
and great things,
the great bursts of love,
random acts of kindness,
tiny shreds of decency

and humane humanity
that pass everyday
across the bridges
of our liquid cities
little towns, countrysides
and yearning, churning
sanguine steel souls…

NUCLEAR WINTER

A Cold War Epilogue

A society now lost
and never to be found
by archaeologists or angels.

A society that concluded itself
with faces all aglow
from the distant light
of the firestorm
burning externally
on the horizon
and eternally
on the curve
of a fragile, fury earth.

An earth,
with missile silos
now empty and silent,
and filling slowly
with the ash
of a fallen society.

An earth,
with grain silos
still full
but their contents
now rotting,
and deadly
to touch and taste.

Silos sitting under
the blackened day skies,
streaked from sea
to unshining sea

with moving gray matter...
the floating entrails
of a people gone mad.

Of a people
for the people
by the people,
but most people
so helpless
to the few,
those fanatic, fateful few
with their frenzied fingers
now melted together
in panic response
to lit up launch buttons
and dangerous deadly discourse.

Those political, fateful few,
leading a civilization
that had become brain dead
to the basics it once had
and should have returned to...

A society of dead faces,
before and after...
now all aglow,
backed up by brains
long gone numb
to the wonders of real life,
and seemingly so deserving
of a fate so horribly,
yet so quickly wrought upon it.

A society,
now laying charred
and forever hot beneath
the deadly falling flakes
of nuclear winter.

MIGRATORY BIRDS

Heading south
and pointed,
those migratory birds,
the mallards, mergansers
and Canada geese.

Together flocks,
those birds,
forming and fanning
dark, distant V-marks
up in the dusking sky
of a late day and
auburn autumn evening.

Color band birds
on a migratory mission,
moving steady on cloud cover currents
like airborne squadrons
in perfect group formation,
flying patient patterned patrol
on watch…
for seed feed targets
and temporary, transitory
sedge shelters.

Sky arrows
those sheen birds,
piercing southbound
and heading warmward…
one field in front,
of the cold approaching
season shift.

SCORCHED HEART POLICY

Did you need to pillage
your visceral village
and then destroy it
in order to save it ???

Did you need to breakdown
a raw recruit romance
and then build it up
in machisma force
like some drill sergeant
looking to mind shape toughness
on such a free flow form ???

Did you wreck like heck
and dwell on "hell"
because of a presumed
non-innocent emotion,
never given a ten second chance,
a two-week notice
or ventured even
a two-bit solution
to spread into something
potentially even fine ???

Are you a lover,
an emoter,
or a pseudo
passion promoter ???

Are you a force feeler,
a miss risk taker,
or just a lip teaser,
a thirst slaker,
in forensic fashion statement ???

Are you but
a drill sergeant,
a thrill sergeant,
a love kill sergeant,
in short black DK dress
with Dior stripes,
looking to put another notch
on your cold gold
Givenchy gun belt ???

NEW YORK CITY STREET VENDOR

That Italian street vendor,
or is he Greek ???
For sure a philosopher king
in miniature, standing round and crownless
by his stainless steel wheel throne,
stopped today
near the overgrown low weeds,
seemingly so out of place
in a city of naked street trees.

That vendor,
smiling all alone
in that lush, sparse street garden,
dispensing wisdom and 'dogs
to the rushing, unmoved masses,
so always on cruise control.

He, standing amongst the steam
of his hot water life pool,
like a swamp preacher,
telling it not like it is
but how it should be.

He, but a propaganda minister,
passing out the public bull,
with the boiling beefs
and those sweet, sweet peppers.

That vendor, vending
and sending out
his daily onioned message,
continually coloring
a city's coloring book,
with mustard yellows,
ketchup reds

John V. LaMotte, Jr.

and relish greens,
and feeding vibrant
the damning day !!!

SPRING START

As the last snow melts
and shadow hidden icicles drip,
as the cold bitter wind diminishes,
Winter loses its grip
and a season finishes.

As the southern birds return
to the sun's heated rays,
trees green
and warm are the winds,
fallen rains
leave a glistening haze
and a new Spring begins.

As an eagle stretches and flies,
the land awakens
with fresh morning dew,
the sun in your eyes,
the beauty of Spring
a reflection of you.

As we walk through
the new slick grass
up on that highest hill,
love warms
my last Winter chill...

A BIRTHDAY IN EAST L.A.

Beginning my 22nd year on earth
in melodramatic March
in warm, sticky dust covered East Los Angeles,
inside a crowded Cerveza Fria tavern
just beyond the corner door,
which is opened wide,
and waiting
for a cool-off night breeze.

The faded pool table
standing solid legged
and centrally low lit,
in the middle
of that dark, dank
beer stank detention hall,
draws my attention call,
as I contemplate my next shot
with the angles
of a pearl-handled pool cue.

The smoke stained mirror
staring cold and sometimes cruel,
behind the varnish laden bar,
also draws my attention
as I contemplate my next year
with the angles
of a dream-candled life view.

A cool breeze, slightly laced
with salty ocean mist,
stops by,
as my imagination, brightly faced
with provocative
seasonal thought patterns,
yearns and dreams anew.

I turn and focus on
the multi-colored number balls,
laying so still and shiny
on the old green table,
as I start to focus on
multi-colored lumber thoughts
for building my new clean year.

Just then,
a violent fight
heat explodes nearby
between a ragged man muttering
and an angry assailant !!!

A long silver switch blade...
gleaming deadly and bright
in the focused pool table light,
flashes fast and close
from a knife in hand
as the eight ball
eyes the corner pocket...

NOVEMBER WOODS

A fallen fog
laying low
over the fallen log
and moving slowly through
November woods,
blurring individual skies
into a single month
of smoky gray.

November woods,
silent, thinned
and graying,
losing fire
and all traces of
October's regal splendor.

But, was it ever there ???
At a glance, November woods
was never really there.

A season's loss of life,
a lost life
in a long, unending season.

A lost sun...
somewhere in the woods,
or maybe no,
a mystery...
until one
or the other goes,
maybe only
November woods knows.

A lost son...
somewhere
in the gray November woods.

A WEDDING BLESSING

Today and beyond...

Dear Lord...

We thank you
for the food on our table
and especially
for the people around it.
Jennifer and John's people.
Real people.
Special people,
who have come together
today, tonight
to celebrate
this joyous joining
this love linking,
this momentous matching
of Jennifer and John.

So Lord...
please bless
this very special occasion
now, and in a way
that the warm, wonderful
flowing feelings
we are experiencing,
last forever
in our hearts and minds
and last for real
throughout the lives
of Jennifer and John.

Lord...
let us rejoice
in the wonders of life,
wonders that sometimes
only become apparent,
so transparent,
so refreshing
and invigorating,
at a wedding,
especially a wedding
of a man and a woman
we know and love.

Lord...
let us
but for a brief moment
experience the silence
now before us...
and think of Jennifer and John,
the two... as one
a fresh start,
their new beginning.

Lord...
bless these two
this one.

Give them laughter
not only on days that are diamonds,
but on days that are stones.

Give them luck,
not in games of chance,
but in their struggle to grow
and always dance
to beautiful wedding music.

And last but not least,
give them
an ever increasing capacity for love...
and continued success
in touching each other's hearts.

EMPTY WINTER TRACKAGE

Out the greasy
fingerprinted windows
of a rocking,
rolling commuter train,
a gray drear day
hangs in over the city.

A drab winter day
with its malevolent sky
dirty snow and
dangerous, ugly black ice,
formed so thick
along the street curbs.

Gray, brown
brick, board buildings
go by,
fast and slow...

Bungalows,
two flats,
three flats,
apartment buildings,
and then
the public housing...
all ebbing and flowing
to the intensity
of the train's velocity,
while the windows,
row on row
street after same street
stare out,
like so many vacant eyes.
And then,
as the rail ride

seems to linger
and lengthen,
it becomes silent,
so very, very silent...
except for the muffled,
rumble cadence
of train on track...

And that's when you can
almost see the blank,
expressionless faces,
of the people standing
along the tracks
and on the bridges,
and when you can almost hear
a lone drummer drumming...
as if a presidential funeral train
pulled by riderless horses
is passing through a city
where nobody cares.

THE WAITRESS IS A WITNESS

The witness was a waitress
up the coffee shop.
The waitress is a witness
who sees a lot,
but mostly hears all,
call out for more
than the Blue Plate Special,
the pungent coffee,
the mac and cheese,
burger and fries
and that heart healthy
gob salad.

She, who heard
and hears more
from the daily gathering,
about life,
about strife,
about the knife
that cuts both ways
across the grain
of our country bread.

She, that waitress
is a witness,
who heard and knows more
than even psychologists
those deep mind divers
who, if you put them all
in one room
and asked them
to give a sense of national direction,
to frame the mood of America,
to tap a trend,
tell it like it is

and maybe even
give a group diagnosis
of the psychosis
of our people,
they would point
every which way
like a bunch of economists,
those self-proclaimed monotonists
who all say different things
and only agree that
the country's economy
is going to hell
in a hand basket
while it's in a brisk recovery !!!

The waitress
in a short span
enters your life,
maybe once
maybe more
if you're a regular.

That waitress,
the friendly, smiling woman
who you can immediately
be friends with,
who usually does her job so well
and helps you through
those high cholesterol,
high fat, high sodium,
over cooked,
preservative packed
bland meals,
while the kids
are bawling
and/or brawling,
and the idiots
in the next booth

are smoking up a storm,
like criminals
facing a firing squad,
maybe it's the same
only slower.

You know
that waitress,
she could be
mom or sis or gram
or the girl next door.
Clean cut, all-American
or maybe not,
there in her white or pink uniform
or black double-knit slacks outfit.
The woman you usually
feel comfortable with
and talk openly with
as she flits from table to table
and back to the kitchen,
to manage her customers proud,
making sure water glasses are full
and the food is hot and fast.

You know them,
these wise women,
even the one with
that wink in her eye,
who flirts,
while she flits
from table to table
to kitchen and back,
and even that occasional
slow food space queen
who smiles and tries
but brings the burger
and forgets the fries,
and holds the onions

but for the guy
two tables down
and not for you.

Yes, the waitress
is our witness,
as we ponder life
in that coffee shop,
that restaurant,
the grill on the corner
and beyond,
and in roadside cafes.

There they are,
that small army
of United States waitresses,
slow or go,
in all shapes and forms,
listening to the chatter
amidst the clatter
of plates and spoons,
and through
the geyser-like steam
of the coffee machine.

There they are, everyday
as life unfolds across the country
over the counters
and around the tables.

The smiles, the trials.
The mood of the country.
The bitchin', the crabbin',
the juicy gossip,
there with your juice and roll.

The pain, the good times,
the bad times,

the lost jobs,
lost homes and farms,
the lost people
the lost direction.

The witness
yes, she is a waitress
up the coffee shop.
Will she soon
write a book
on table mat papers,
the ones stained
with coffee, ketchup
and tears ?

Will she tell all she saw
but mostly heard word for word,
and send our President,
a copy with his coffee,
so he can wake up
and know who America's people are...

GROWTH CYCLES

Don't you get it,
something good is trying to grow ???

Will you not build boxes
or fortress foundations around it,
or brain contain
its movement,
freeze its flow,
question its content
and suspiciously eye its intent,
or make reference
to the still rough edges
of its moment...
and only let it go,
allow it to
expand geometrically,
exponentially, horizontally
and vertically...
and even emotionally,
naturally and so free
in an order that is organized
in a chaotic way,
organically
with no pesticides
or even preservatives ???

Can you just let it happen
and test your restraint
not to paint it into a corner,
but watch only instinctively,
rather than react conservatively
to something good
that could maybe just go on,
that's got to move out and up
and move forward

John V. LaMotte, Jr.

in a free, free way,
maybe with a mad, mad momentum ???

Will you stop and watch
and let this something grow,
without multiple fears
or quicksilver tears,
without remorse or repugnance,
but truly watch
with open eyes and ears
and open hands,
mind and heart,
keen on what
will break routine
of the easy,
the comfortable,
the known,
seen everyday
on your personal screen,
ready and willing
for your life to change
a little, or maybe even
drastically and dramatically
in a pure, positive
and passionate sense ???

Something good is trying to grow,
will you let it, let it go ???

WIND LISTENING

Thinking deeply...
and talking to yourself,
going inbound
and looking
at who you are
now and before
and maybe tomorrow...
and wind listening.

Exploring inner thoughts
and feelings,
for where to go
to find out what you will be
what you will see
there in your telescope eye
exploring internally
and externally
and wind listening.

Touching your heart
to feel your emotions
to see how emotions affect you,
while searching your soul
and asking yourself
what to do,
how to live
and why...
and wind listening.

John V. LaMotte, Jr.

Challenging your mind
to future revelations,
disclosures
and insights…
you then listen
to that wild, whistling
wandering wind...
whispering
as it tells you all.

A BIRTHDAY CARD FOR PAT-HEART

Another birthday...
much different from the rest,
yet thank God,
just like all the rest...
the family, the friends,
the flowing feelings.

Another birthday,
is just a moment's pause
in our fast lane life pulse,
to remember
to stop all in the now,
and to listen to you,
and to see you,
and hear you,
and touch you...
wherever you may be.

But no...
a real pause
is not necessary
to witness thoughts
that run on and on,
in constant steady stream,
through a kindred heart span.

No, a birthday
is only a happening,
an event, coming and going.

Maybe a simple moment,
out of a complicated day,
a moment's pause...
is all that is needed,
to apply delineation,

to what is always stored
and recharging
as life goes on.

In high speed
time and motion,
but a moment's pause...
and its delineation,
sharpens our focus
on one who has loved
and is so very much
loved in return.

BUFFALO GRASS

What of the Buffalo Grass...
and tangential time ?

Does it matter
to be in sync...
or completely focused
like a Nikon shooter
waiting and maneuvering
for that perfect shot,
while missing a lot ?

What of the coffee stain
hiding in the carpet strands,
known but to you
and the whispering fish
looking at it every day
in the light throw
of their tight tank ?

Who cares ?
Who's perfect ?
Is there anything anywhere
or someone somewhere
really perfect ?
A Mercedes,
a Rolex,
Godiva Chocolate,
Hagen Dazs,
A Super Bowl ring,
Breakfast at Tiffany's,
A Room at the Ritz,
Paris in the Spring ?
Rob and Laura,
Country Club Republicans,
Mr. Clean,

John V. LaMotte, Jr.

Mr. and Mrs. Cleaver,
Sheriff Andy Taylor,
Miss America,
Mr. Universe,
His Airness,
Her Highness,
The Pope ?
Yes, but no
he'll be the first
to tell you so,
that there is Buffalo Grass
in even the Vatican's crisp clipped lawn,
and red blood in blue blood
no matter how much ivy
grows on brick walls.

A pearl button
missing from
your French silk shirt ?
Too much to handle,
or too good to be true...
the fabric
the look
it's you!!!

So lighten up
and cut yourself some slack.

Are straight A's,
straight teeth,
seamless gutters,
gold bouillon soup
and wrinkle-free khakis
even legal ???

AUGUST TUNDRA HELL

The sun... at new morning
was already high and hot
and early on forecasting
an all day and probably
a pending week
of August tundra hell.

By noon that peak pointed sun
was a brilliant white burst
you dared not look at...
and by then the heat
had become ungodly,
hanging heavy and furnace-like
in the stifling, stagnant air,
of what could have been
a wet west desert
within a northern jungle zone.

There was no escaping
that bitter, radiating radish heat,
like in annual winter
in cold pack places,
when you can layer on more clothes
and move around to fight off
the attacking racking cold.

No, the heat...
you couldn't escape it,
here, there
anywhere or anyway,
as it drained you, the dogs
and the recharge fields
of bodily liquids
and desperate energy.

To quench the nagging thirst,
you inhaled water
like a horse head
in a road side trough,
drinking and drinking
until your stomach bulged
and the bloat only compounded
your heat seeking misery.

You prayed for some wind,
even the slightest of breeze
to invade that desert/tropics zone,
and then when wind finally arrived
it brought only blasts
of hotter, tighter air.

In continuum flow...
salt lick sweat poured out
from every micro-pore
of your thin body skin,
and like you,
everything else
was moist and dank
from the cut thick humidity,
as the house and furniture
seemed to be sweating too.

You longed for rayless night,
its sub-darkness and assumed cool.
Yet later, though the sun was long gone,
it was still a lot hot
and sleep was near impossible
in that August tundra hell.

BINDING QUESTIONS WITH KNOW ANSWERS

A Four-Act Play for the Love Challenged

<u>Act 1: One Night Stand</u>
Brought together on a lonely night...
or was it a lonely day that slipped away ???

Together with each other
yet, still alone... empty.

Together for what ???
Companionship, someone to talk to, to love,
and/or make love to ???

It's cold and midnight blue,
will we make it through...
the lonely night...
to the lonely day
only to part
and go each other's way ???

<u>Act 2: Cold Fusion</u>
In our fast-paced world,
you are mellow intrusion...
you seem to make so much
comfortable, common sense
in a complex, complicated
world of confusion.

Are you really real,
or are we just a cold fusion ???

Act 3: Song of Indecision
Can we go on from today,
must we stop going on this way ???

Should we end
and start anew
like a cloudless sky blue...
after stormy weather...
should we part
or be together ???

Is there love left today ???
Should I leave
or should I stay ???
What do you want,
what do you say ???

Is it yes,
or is it no ???

Let's let go
and let's be free,
you with you
and I with me.

But, it's seems not right
to be alone by day
alone by night.

Do you need me,
do I need you ???
No... but yes
I guess we do ???

Act 4: Strangers in the Night
Why kid ourselves
or anyone else ???

We aren't fooling anyone.
We are just fools,
pretending to love,
pretending to care,
trying to live
pretending to share.

To share what,
the same house,
the same bed
the same air ???

Apart we are alive
but together dead.
With such emptiness
and no real deal feelings,
aren't we just
beautiful strangers
going through
the movie motions ???

The End ???

HATE & HOPE

The death masks
hanging up there
in the thin urban air,
on gang sign walls,
on rusting chain link fences
on broken hoop poles,
invisible, but not divisible.

The eyeless death masks
up there, stare
at the heart smile children
so down... down below,
playing their good ground games
with taped up balls of hope
and society sticks of hate,
amidst their own
and only laughter
and the pop pop
of the daily gang gunfire.

Under the death masks
those innocent children play,
so clean in deed
and so deep deep in need.

Heart smile children,
who may survive,
but do not thrive
as they contemplate
the day, some way,
that spirited people, someone
will pull the death masks down,
curse the masks
and crush them
into powdery pieces,

and use them
to mulch change
the broken land,
that dark corner of a place,
that neighborhood,
a neighborhood
the children must call home.

MONTH OF SUNDAYS

A woman prays and prays
for many nights, many days.

She loses a parent to cancer,
and prays and prays.

She is poor and lonely
but still prays,
and marries a man
she shouldn't have.
She stays
and just as poor,
she prays.

She loses a son to war
and she prays on.

She loses a daughter to drugs
and still poor, prays
while her husband drinks.

Bills stack
she has a heart attack
and prays.

Her hands ache
her eyes dim
she continues to pray.

And then one day,
she forgets her prayers
and dies...
a painless, peaceful death.

MOON TALK ON A DAILY BASIS

Those combinatorial
conversational prerogatives
that they spill and speak
in such tech speak
or is it tech talk
or just double-talk ?

Isn't it all maybe even triple talk ?
Or linguistic lubrication at best,
and at worst...
convoluted communication,
meant to express
or is it impress
or really depress
with long complicated words
a few simple thoughts ???

Prosecutorial,
spousal programs,
quantum tunneling,
drag coefficient,
parlayed initiative,
a reciprocal agreement...
(resulting in yet another attention deficit)
synchronized contingencies,
parallel modular outputs,
locomotory support platforms,
quadrupled ingress/egress aperture,
strategic memoranda (a memo),
tactical resolution (deadly force),
deadly force (killed someone),
adverse weather visibility device (a windshield wiper),
nutritional avoidance therapy (a diet),
dynamic inactivity (huh?),
an involuntary dismount (thrown from a horse),

a tactical exchange of nuclear weapons
(is there any other way ?).

A surgical strike (with pinpoint accuracy),
physical containment,
a station adjustment,
an escalated disturbance by hostile groups (a riot),
a non-ecological boundary (a fence),
that canine seclusion habitat,
but Rover's dog house...
an unplanned inventory reduction,
but a fire in the factory !!!

Synthetically synthetic syntax
or a wacky worldwide
word slide lingo explosion ???
Etc. etc.
vis-à-vis
and quid pro quo,
or no,
should I say
"Let me say this about that",
but all of this that is said about that,
is nothing more (or less)
than a double-barreled, rapid fire,
AK-47 long clip, short burst,
barrage of verbiage
pouring in at 120 miles per hour,
like hockey pucks (semi-rigid polyemic disks)
coming straight at you
without your conversational goalie mask on,
resulting in a tactical exchange
of nuclear wordisms...
directly in your face !!!

That exchange,
but a range of lengthy
usually unnecessary

debate enhancing syntax,
shaped and spoken
and sometimes salaciously spit
by corporate, legal, bureaucratic,
military and/or professorial types,
released into the air
and into the sound chamber
of the inner ear
as eccentric,
often egomaniacal
explanatory enterprise,
in the disguise
of the pseudo-wise
trying to articulate,
illuminate and sometimes
even enunciate
minor points,
short thoughts
or simple ideas
with too many
floodlight wonder words
and sky search sentences,
an overkill...
if you will.

A parley or litany
of long, lazy languorous words
heard individually
yet all together
as daily deadly dialectic diatribes
of those who like
to verbally spar and joust
for the sake
(and the need)
of hearing the sound
of their own voice
running on empty
and running on...

these rhetorical Rambos
fueled by global globules
of lung air
and perpetuated
by the air
in their inflated heads (big egos)
adding more and more
major, yet insignificant
non-essential time wasting words
and slick shaped sentence structures,
delivered in staccato
boring, bony banter,
that monotone monologue,
that exhausting exhortation
of wild eyed Type A types
on jargon jags
in dueling debates.

This discourse intercourse
of bombastic boors
and/or bombed bores,
delivering soliloquies,
handing out harangues
and torrential tirades
fueled by those lugubrious lungs
and sometimes the venting of spleens...

Enough already !!!
of those salivating
foam fleck mouthed
humanoid word processors,
with their silver tech talk tongues
and floppy disc dementia,
those with most excellent
self-olfactory output capabilities
who were born with
the wrong manufacturers equipment
of puffery, pomposity, pontification

and some even demagoguery.

We are badgered and
now brilliantly bored
with the exponential growth
of their words and
on-going verbal assault,
with this overeager
expression explosion,
resulting in our own
awesome attention deficit
over this burgeoning,
daily street filibuster.

All this aggravated articulation
and complicated communication,
this dangerous diction doublespeak,
this gargantuan, gargled and garbled gobbledygook,
is nothing but simple, overdone, overblown
out of proportion bull doo !!!

Say what ???

The End...
(the mandatory and necessary, yet possibly temporary
conclusion of this pseudo-eloquent, elocution electrocution)

THE WARDEN

On the rock, the Warden
in his solitary confinement
inside himself
in internal incarceration.

Thirty days in the hole,
plus extended day time
for intended night pasts
with no time off even for good behavior.

Locking himself up in lock down,
sentencing himself to self-imposed exile,
somewhere in his inner Siberia,
where it is so very bitter cold
and where snowfall
functions as a jail coolant
for a flaming furnace heart.

Sentenced to life on death row,
within a multitude rack of human cells,
lined up in blocks
with no steel shuttered doors.

In his cerebral guard tower
in that skin-walled prison,
he sits so secure,
with mental machine guns
always on guard.

So vigilant and watchful,
the Warden,
for personal transgression
or regression to a passionate past.

The Warden,

sitting there behind the desk
in his leather strapped electric chair,
never again to lead into temptation,
never again to commit a non-crime of passion
and never once asking the governess
for a pardon.

John V. LaMotte, Jr.

CANDLED OPERA

Candles,
at any time
in the sin
but not in the sun
or whenever dark.

Candles,
even in mind meadows,
find shadows
somewhere up there
just below
the cloud cover
and drip line
of the tall pine
etched across the
rock mountain flanks.

Cord cut
paraffin poles,
stacked side by side
on end and burning,
send skyward
light smoke
and smoked light
from hot tips,
like barkless
ringless, melt trees
non-giant, cylindrical
and symmetrical.

Candles,
but straight stick
tight tentacles,
vertical and all,
and multiplied

by ten in a row
like laser lipped
logarithms
in geometric progression,
yet often free form
and lava like
in comparison,
when seen together
the individual flames
are volcanic flow slip
on automatic slow drip.

Hard, soft smooth stalks,
enflamed with
the momentary spark
of match heads,
whose sulfur skin faces
were scraped against
the charcoal beard
of a fire pack.

Candles,
separate thin spark shoots,
that gathered together
become a micro day forest,
a wax woods... flame orchards,
that bring incredible light
to anyone's darkness
and even to someone's sadness
and lack of emotional oxygen.

Together, these drip tips
power power outs,
those light loss incidents,
when darkness can only
be sung to
and illuminated
by the passion crescendo
of your candled opera.

DREAM DEPRIVATION

Dream deprivation...
that lonesome period,
in the ebb and flow
of salt sweet dream waters.

A sleeper's slump,
with false fantasy starts,
that dreaded night
when lights go out
and eyes close,
when fantasies, dreams,
crystallizing hopes
and self-induced revelations,
no longer seem believable,
valid or even possible,
when one enters
into a time frame,
that is void
of internalized vision activity,
when sleep...
only replenishes the Z count
while doing nothing
to reinvigorate the mind,
heart, soul or spirit.

LONELY WINTER LOVE LETTER

He enters the Northern House
released from winter's bloody ice grip,
his face red-white with wind bite,
his hands deep cold and circulatory numb.

The fresh logged fire
stoked in the hearth,
flames not yet full,
welcomes him,
as does the almost empty
bottle of golden whiskey
standing in thick dust
on the oak mantle beam.

He sits quietly in the overstuffed chair,
alone in the solid black night
without her, there
in the heavy darkness at fire front,
writing and warming
writing and sipping,
and watching the flames
climb and grow....

Then, like the fine whiskey,
the floating, flickering fire
goes slowly, slowly down,
and its soft dancing wall images
shadow shake the darkening room...
until the last fire chunk
falls spitting and hissing into
the gray white ashes...
"And you know,
those flames and glowing coals
can last forever in one's mind, especially
when the Northern House is empty.

John V. LaMotte, Jr.

And you know,
that thick wool sweater
that you made me,
that you gave me,
keeps me warm
when you are gone.

But, you know,
it can get awfully cold,
when the Winter Wind Lion is bold
and the fire is too old to see,
and when I'm without you...
and all alone with me."

MOMENTARY J. MAN

A night like the other night,
for one great moment
weren't we something ???
When for a single man and single woman
it was but a single, simple moment together,
it was one long song during a short night out
on the Toddlin' Town,
dancing and laughing like never before,
like a haunting music score,
pouring up and out the street floor
through you to me electrically,
like a crossfire caught between us,
ignited by the black white staccato
of a fast piano there before us
and the sweet metal sound
of a slow silver sax,
wailing close,
but distant and sensual outside
somewhere unseen
in that background night.

For a fleeting moment
in our short simple lives,
a transitory, temporary love song
played exclusively,
yet so elusively
for one cool blues man,
seemingly welded together
with a sparking torch
to one hot jazz lady...

John V. LaMotte, Jr.

GRANDMA'S NIGHTMARES

Asleep in her lace place room
near me down the hall,
where the guardian angle
of the night light
reaches through her door
and across the floor,
touching simple treasures
and eclectic furniture
as it meets the drape cut moonlight
at the foot of her bed.

Grandma, in there
in her silver, sometimes troubled sleep,
with that occasional cry out
softly crying out amongst
the very close in silence
of a sleeping family house.

So startling then
when it breaks
the silence night,
that quasi-scream
of elderly
in troubled sleep.

Startling then
that sound,
when she cries out
for senior safety
after so long
an unsafe city life,
after so many
late work hours,
dark alleys and vestibules,
broken street lights

and the time tension
of her daily cleaning life.
A lonesome period,
sometimes the naught night.
Even more so than her senior days
long away from us.

Those quiet nights,
when her eyes shut slowly,
and she couldn't see us,
and could only hear
the banging of tree arms against
mind rattling windows.

Those nights,
when hands folded in blue vein clutch,
clenched each other in prayer
and/or for some touch and comfort
to ward off the bad spirits
of being alone.

And then that sound again,
that soft cry out,
a call out
traveling at me
down the connective hall,
like a sound muffled
short nightmare sequence.

That quasi-scream again,
in her later years
when her day is gone
and she is left alone
in the darkness of sleep,
to cry out against
those lurking night frights
some false,
some real.

Those limited day views,
there in her cloudy
yet still sparkling eyes,
getting so muddled later
in her troubled silver sleep
when she cries out for senior safety
after so long an unsafe city life.

HOUSE & GARDEN BEAUTIFUL

The house was absolutely incredible.
It was designed, built, decorated
and maintained
like no other house
you had ever seen.

Outside,
the expansive, expensive lawn
was so meticulously tailored,
chemicalled and manicured,
that you wondered
if anyone ever stepped on it,
or if a weed ever dared to grow,
or if Fido and Fifi ever dared
to do their dutiful duty there ???

Inside the house,
everything too,
was so perfectly organized,
orchestrated, arranged
and aligned,
immaculately clean
and seemingly so new.

Even the daily newspaper,
was arranged just so
on the sparkling, smudge free
low glass table,
so proper there,
next to the Wall Street Journal,
French architecture books
and glossy magazines
about gentry living.

It was a house so beautiful,
that you didn't even want
to put anything in a garbage can
if you could find one.

A place,
where you were afraid
you might track a speck of dirt
onto the snow white carpeting,
or where you dared not sit
on the tucked, tufted sofa
so you wouldn't muss
the proper stacking
of the multi-colored accent pillows,
or use the toilet paper,
because it was so scented
and embossed,
and corner folded
in just that certain way,
and God forbid...
create an unpleasant odor
in the bathroom,
for it might upset
the special fragrance balance
permeating the air,
from the fresh cut flowers,
rosewood chips
and perfumed shower drapes.

Yes, it was a house
so beautiful and perfect,
that it was very uncomfortable,
and you knew people lived there,
but you wondered where ???

GRAFFITI GODS

Tall jerk ponies
released, rejected
or is it ejected
from the Detox Center
on South Kedzie,
after doing time
for being jacked up
and injected.

The jerk ponies
and graffiti gods,
doing deals in front
of the expressionist paintings
on the brick walls
of virulent viaducts
under the Expressway.

Do you call it all
graffiti?
Or is it agony art,
or maybe urban outrage
expressed in cruel calligraphy
visually, but still violently
so outside the gilded cage
of the Gold Coast ???

The jerk ponies,
graffiti gods
and street reverends,
after doing time
for buzzing brains,
stand a dime a dozen
with gold chains
in front of half-way houses,
wrong way signs,

liquor stores,
storefront churches
and every corner bar.

Those street reverends,
but former graffiti gods,
now preaching
and leaching
green blood
and golden spirit
from those basic folks
with nothing more to give
and nothing left to lose.

A sting of ray, a sting,
lighting the way
but only for neo-witch doctors
who curse the city geography
not covered by the dark shadows,
where periodic light filters
send pseudo-crab warriors
into a frenzy
of threatening
yet theatrical moves,
where most of these
jammers and scammers
are hooked on tubes
of chemical
and political life support
from the suits downtown,
who eventually
always give way
to public sway.

Is there life
in this 'hood
after death of spirit
and not only bod,

when there's lack of god,
no matter what shape or form
he or she may take
or where came from,
except of course
the graffiti deity ???

You can't put pistols
in the hands
of those graffiti gods,
for you be gone
and bought the farm,
once you get past
the sick street charm
of a suave city
storefront sermon.

After local loss of breath
temporarily
or permanently,
why ask why ???

COLDWATER WOMAN

In a coldwater flat
in a coldwater town,
fresh Spring mud
lays stiff and semi-frozen,
like road custard
spread thick after
the run-off rain rides
the weed ditches
that separate asphalt lanes
from farm fields.

Before that rain
hits the ground running,
it becomes cold,
and seeps through
the sky cracks
in building roofs,
seen but to a naked eye
and a naked woman,
laying flat and warm
in that coldwater flat,
laying still and steaming
in the temperate air,
like the town road custard.

That coldwater woman,
dodging the rain's cold water,
that precedes the frozen freeze.
Semi-sweet to taste,
the wet, wet streamers
invading those sky cracks
and dripping down
and slowly slick across
each impervious pore
of her water-cooled body.

BORDER WARS

The city limits,
but invisible fences
there in your mind field,
installed like thin, linear tank traps
around a tender turf
that changes government hands
in your passion nation
like lands belonging
to ideologue leader dogs.

Those mystical municipal borders
so around you,
delineated by the wizardry
of a city planner
or at least drawn
in invisible pen and ink
by a careless cartographer,
who defined your geographic region
and corresponding psychic space
as a secret mind place
that defies even Boolean logic.

Bold bucolic boundaries
out in the country
at the county line,
laying somewhere sight unseen
in fields that extend
way beyond your imagination.

Those limits
as edges there,
to find and redefine
when traveling to and from
your cozy closed community.

Those razor sharp mental borders,
but invisible
and invincible wailing walls,
that keep nothing out
but only you in.

LANDMARK STATUS

Drive through
the West Side,
north or south
of Roosevelt Road,
into Lawndale,
a neighborhood
but a cruel caricature,
a carved carcass
of its former fine self.

A neighborhood
now emptied of
so many people
and so many buildings,
those memory places.

What walls remain,
stand open like
community ribs
foregone of flesh,
the windowless halls
but hate holes
staring out and down,
at the shattered glass
and shattered lives
so scattered about
the gaping, rat-wide
foundation cracks,
rotten ethnic lumber floors,
deadly powder people....
and that once dog.
Drive through
and that big dog
you will find there,
the one that lives

dead on its side,
laying flat
and one eye fixed
on the occasional
copper paper cinder
rising from the nearby
garbage can fires.

That dog,
Lying so stiff legged
in a brackish oily curb pool,
that fills in during long rain
or broken hydrant flush,
all the rough run-off
of a jagged, tire-tracked slumscape.

In advanced state
of rigor mortis,
still staring endlessly
to the sky
from that broken,
street side pain pool,
that big dog
that dead dog,
but a small city statue,
a landmark
in a marked land.
A cruel symbol
of the blight
and gone hope
so there all around it.

That dog,
temporarily preserved
alongside a street
like a statue
in a once fine city park,
there for all who dare

to go and see.

A stilled landmark,
no longer engaged
in terrestrial dogfights,
that once dog,
that now symbol,
no longer on rat patrol
in back alleys,
hunting for desperate food
with desperate people
like a crazed urban wolf,
that dog,
now momentarily there
as a statue
for all who dare
to go and see.

That dog,
that canine cadaver,
a landmark in a marked land,
temporarily preserved
by the grim city taxidermist,
who lurks amongst
the cratered streets,
rutted alleys
and fallen windowless bricks
of Lawndale.

PRE-STORM WARNING

Early evening rainstorm,
gathering on distant August sky,
somewhere out behind
a seeking mountain range.

The true day begins to darken,
as its light source
slowly leaves the moving horizon,
glowing playfully in and out
of the fast approaching strong clouds.

The true day
and its normal subject matter
stops… is forgotten and now warm
in a very different way.
And so fragrant with the blossom scent
of the flower garden vines
hanging vibrant
over every uneven fence line.

A special silence
slowly pervades the senses, except
for the frantic background chirping
of the day birds
hidden way back
in the mountain maples.

This warm silence,
a rare, short length time
to contemplate so freely and clearly,
to absorb as much as you can quickly,
of the fleeting soft sensation
of that peaceful calm,
before a late Summer storm
that temporal quiet…

a sensual seasonal tranquility.

It is then, that those long strong clouds
crash collide just above you,
and the now truculent,
turbulent sky space,
sting lit by lightning shrapnel
crackles and explodes
with boom box thunder,
and the reversed cooling sensation
of a powerful Summer rain,
suddenly prevails !!!

EULOGY FOR THE GOOD WITCH

She didn't die,
but must have
melted down
or vanished back then,
somewhere in your thin early air,
or just moved on years ago,
that good witch...
and all the subsequent
good witches.

A dream queen
that good witch,
at homecoming and prom
and probably beyond.

A child woman back then,
so filled with yesterday's
puppy lust.

A good witch,
long gone and good-bye,
and melted,
into that pool
of heady youth dew.

Gone on for real
to a lust that lasts,
down yellow brick roads
that must have led
to a true emerald city,
with munchkins
and white picket fences...

That good witch
way back then,
leaving you the wizard, behind
to love all those bold
and beautiful bad witches.

HEM HOUSE

In the treeless highlands,
in the entry portal
above charcoal slate floor and
timber thick ceiling,
within a long, lean frame,
hung a huge portrait
of Max and Katrina.
Their likeness was stunning,
the brushed body colors
so vibrant and alive.

Up there in that special house,
they looked down upon you
from that entrance painting
like cruelly matched characters
in an old hard cover,
thick page Hemingway novel,
all yellow, musty
and lusty.

The dark-eyed,
mustachioed man
and beautiful, buxom woman,
mysterious and sensual,
deep and demanding.

They looked down upon you,
in a haunting way,
as if they were in the first row
at the bullfights in Pamplona....
and you were the fighter of bulls !!!
These two,
this coupling,
seemed so destined
to be there on the wall,

in fiction,
and for real
in that Hemingway house,
transcribed up there
under a clay tile roof
set low and rippled
amongst the rolling, cattled hills.

A solid crafted structure
terrestrial and stone strong.
A fortress,
against wicked storms,
interlopers
and the sometimes
darkness of their day.

A passion palace,
built for love making,
and the cultivation
of children, crops and power.

That house,
way up there
in the treeless highlands,
a Hemingway house,
a place to come to
to be proud of
a place to die in...
and for.

PARDON ME, A PRISONER'S PLEA

Ex-President Richard Nixon pardoned September 8, 1974

A man commits a crime
that affects a few,
is punished
and should be.

A President commits a crime
that affects millions,
is not punished
and should be ???

The President is pardoned today.
It is said
that disgrace and humiliation
are enough.

The man is not pardoned today
or tomorrow
yet society says he too
must experience
disgrace and humiliation.

The man's crime is small...
this is bad.

The man's crime is large...
this is terrible.

The President's crime
small or large
is terrible,
for he is the trusted leader
of a country, of the free world.

The truth
of Presidential wrongdoing...
must be known
when there is a breach
of national responsibility and trust.

But, we must not talk of this
after all he was the President,
the leader of the land...
pardon me
for I am just a man.

HARVEST HEART

A farmwoman, farmer
a woman of fertile earth,
eye bright and summer sunned
beneath smooth brim hat
and behind bleached blue denim.
Alone on awesome acres,
and so proud.

So quietly
and longingly proud...
of her lithe love garden
and plowed passion rows,
so easy to seed,
and of her soft,
cultivated firm fields
so easy to reach,
touch and pick.

And so proud
of her prairie path,
cleared and clean,
and winding
through her private countryside,
a silk soaked soil land.
A path winding and turning
yet leading so easily...
to her always unlocked front door,
and her pending hopeful harvest.

ICE STATION CHICAGO

A powerful ice storm
lashing out across Lake Michigan
cold cocks Chicago at midnight
swiftly, silently,
then stops snow suddenly...

And the night glow neighborhoods
deep asleep on the Lake's edge,
are encased in rippled ice sheets
and freeze framed.

The brick and stone structures,
giant willow whips,
paver walks and lampposts
all shining together
like mini-castle clusters,
under a sorcerer's clear cake glazing,
all stiff and glossy
in a cold night gap,
seemingly a time warp
with no animated people.

A surreal setting
this diamond hard night,
shining glossy and slick,
stopped and on hold, except
for the gray white sewer ghosts,
dancing schizoid
to the irregular beat
of the low street wind
and occasional passing car.
Nightglow neighborhoods,
lining the Lake lip,
temporarily under the spell
of a wily weather wizard...

iced down
and storm frozen,
and for a brief midnight moment,
preserved...
like grand brick pheasants
under crystal winter glass.

SOCIAL WORKER BURNOUT

Those social worker eyes...
so special, so soft
and so searing,
reveal now
that they have lost it all,
after many years
of putting together
so many broken lives.

Those eyes,
burn no more
in social outrage,
and focus no more
on the terrible injustices,
the lack of harmony
and/or the inequity
so permanently lodged
in society's underbelly.

The eyes...
those eyes,
stare hollow
and empty now,
like those of your former clients
long gone and maybe not forgotten...
the day/night drug daze
of gangbanger punks
wired on junk by 11am,
or the blank, brutalized look
of welfared mothers,
awaiting eviction
and husband
simultaneously,
or the sweet stone stare
of the lonely, hungry elderly

who have given up hope...

That's it !!!
The quixotic enthusiasm,
that almost zealous fervor,
that almost religious hope,
is now gone from you too...
jettisoned somewhere
with your lance and sword
back on the broken streets
of diseased and dying neighborhoods.

And now, burnout has ascended,
like a built up immunity
from the repeated daily injections
of *"the last, the lowest, the lost and the least"*.

And now, a thick crust of scar tissue
has formed over that once bleeding heart.
A sarcastic, cynical tissue,
masking too, a soul,
rusted down over the years
in an internal place
where idealism once shined
in dewy-eyed patina.

And with burnout,
an ironic impatience has evolved,
not only for a convoluted social service system
and cruel set society,
but for the kids, the seniors, the poor,
and the clutching and grabbing
and clinging of their dirty hands...
hands you once held tightly
for so many hours.
Those eyes...
and those healing hands
reach out no more.

Gone forever dry
are the professional
and personal tears
usually shed internally…
and alone…

The streets and the lives
in those nasty negative neighborhoods
are now so empty of you…

Dedicated to John, my late father and Patti, my sister… two great social workers… based on their recollections in our kitchen, late one night and long ago, of lost social workers in a socially lost world.

STAY TUNED

A touching...
with lighthearted moments
that have at times,
run deep and hard
like momentary sun mirrors
on rapid canyon rivers.

A reaching...
in very short time span,
with periodic analysis
into the sensual unknown
and make believe
desire future.

A wondering...
sometimes fleeting,
yet, slowly filling
with fresh intrigue,
like a vineyard
and its growing
wine yield.

A gaining...
of momentum
in a stop-start mind frame,
an exciting heart game
that so continues on...

MIDDLE AMERICA

Black loamed soil soul.
Horizontal heart tissue,
with asphalt arteries
and cornstalk sinew,
so rowed, ready
and reaching.

Beautiful skin fields,
the flatland plains.
Sometimes wheated,
often low bushed
and/or sparse treed.
The majestic wind wave tall grass
so always clean
and vibrant green.

A gentle, quiet strength
this place, these people
with rock rough dignity
and feet planted firmly on
and in the earth,
yet with eyes always searching
the prairie star skies.

Commerce crossroads,
cool, calm, conservative,
always thinking
and sometimes leaping.

Rarely tragic,
sometimes magic.
Bread and butter,
meat and potatoes.
Basic, solid and neighborly,
willing to lend a steady hand

John V. LaMotte, Jr.

to share a strong, stable land.

A rolling land of subtle beauty,
seemingly endless, seamless
and somewhat surreal.
A prairie place
that seems to go on
into ranged horizons…almost forever.

A prairie pulse, this place
a country's core and conscience,
America's heartland.

OAK LOG FIRES

New oak log fires
in old charred hearths,
like old men with young hearts.

A deep-rooted strength
the oak wood,
even when wind chapped,
chopped and chunked
for fire.

Stately aristocratic trees
leading long lives
of dark green splendor
sometimes leave their lives
in a short span sight blaze,
a seemingly eternal flaming
there above the fresh great weight
and sweet, wet smell
of solid oak wood.

New oak fires,
bright and stark
in the dark, dark hearth,
are but old forests
in different conclusion.

A master's ancient landscape tool,
fallen flat on forest floors,
a chopped and chunked
flame fuel,
so fine all aglow.

IN REMISSION ???

Can one bash
the senses
such that
no amount of
extracurricular activity
or nouveau romantic pressure
can surgically repair,
stitch mend,
recycle or replace
that which is fading
or maybe even gone ???

Could it return
or reinvigorate
or reincarnate
in another life form,
with a different facade,
such that there
is renewal,
vim and vigor
accompanied
by true change
and awesome progress ???

Is it gone,
will it last forever,
or will it go into
romantic remission,
only to return
in a way
that drives one and two on,
and on,
and on,
like a powerful
local emotion engine

that needs not petrol,
but only a steady flow
of unpasteurized,
unrefined true love
to fuel it ???

PATIENCE

Waiting...
in a line,
always a long slow-go line...
at the grocery store,
a movie theater,
a "fast food" joint
an unemployment office,
in a damn traffic jam... gridlock!!!

Waiting...
always waiting,
to develop from raw rookie
to seasoned veteran,
to grow from small child
to big adult,
for that first chin whisker,
for that first drop of womanhood.

Waiting...
for crop rain to fall,
for wet rain to cease.

Waiting...
for the sun to go down
and deep sleep to begin,
for sunrise
and waking moments,
for night to come
and hide what is the day,
for day to arrive
and illuminate
the lurking dangers
of mind darkness.

Waiting...

for a lover who will return,
for a lover who won't,
for a lover that never was.

Waiting...
for that phone call
for those test results,
positive or negative,
pass or fail,
promoted or not,
for acceptance,
for recognition,
a pat on the back,
for arrivals and departures
temporary or forever,
for the mail
a fax
an email,
the information.

Waiting for a love letter
a greeting card
a Valentine
an announcement
a good-bye note,
a rejection notice.

Waiting...
nine months to be born,
four years for the next election,
two weeks until payday
fifteen minutes for fame,
and a lifetime to die...
while waiting patiently
at the sky roofed station
for a dream train...
that's running late.

PARIS EYES

And how that artist
in the Montmarte art district
up on the point hill
high above that exquisite city,
pencil sketched you...
with such accuracy,
freezing your image
in warm, hard flashes
of thick pencil lead,
sketched light to the touch
as if the ghost of a master
was guiding his hand.

Yet, the French pastel gray
was but a smear,
because he couldn't see the depth
of the naked perimeter canvas
or the distant somewhere you...

Or could he see the real you,
as he engraved into that portrait
in fine line wash,
your look and likeness...
those liquid eyes...
burning dark, animate holes
in the taut white fabric
and the free Paris morning.

And how he couldn't see
the depth of you
or could he,
as he seemed to capture
in his mind's eye
your eyes...
that haunting image,

that love look,
that deep stunning stare,
I want to see
everyday, everywhere,
reflected in a you
somewhere out there
in that fine Paris air.

STILLBIRTH

He was a man,
who had died,
shortly after being born.

Yet his heart beat on...
his static life,
suspended in animation,
on-hold,
barely breathing,
frozen and stopped,
yet moving on...

His was a life,
seemingly void of emotion,
like a living death.
No emotion,
for a mother and father
who had created him
and loved him,
for a wife
he only pretended to love,
for his four children,
his job, his daily existence.

A quasi-suppressed anger,
possibly the only emotion
ever expressed, occasionally,
when the television was broken
or he was out of smokes or beer.

He seemed to exist,
in name only,
on a checkbook,
on credit cards,
on a mortgage,

as a man
who went through
the daily 9 to 5 motions,
only to hook up each evening
to his television life support system
after eating a dinner
he never tasted...

CATHERINE CATHEDRAL

She reminded you oddly enough
of a magnificent European cathedral.
Grand, tall and elegant,
richly embellished
and well crafted... of stone.

A beautiful womanplace,
where some people worshipped inside
and too many worshipped outside.

Where candles were purposely lit
with good intentions,
yet burned only briefly.

A place where light shined gloriously
through stained glass fashion colors,
only to be so darkened by her night.

An open place,
where most activity was concentrated
in brief magical moments of season
and the quiet pageantry of hope,
where white laced choirs,
gold piped music
and hosannas rang out...
and then were still.

And yet, a closed place
where silence and darkness
rested so often, in agony...
behind the finely carved doors,
after the small red glows of the altar candles,
went out with the external day worshippers.

Sadly, Catherine was a cathedral,
a magnificent structure
which often housed
only silence and darkness...
and the occasional chanting of a night priest,
trying to reach her inner sanctum.

NIGHT BLANKET

A fabric night,
textured and soft
and laying over us
like a rough-cut,
pre-washed
designer blanket,
there for us to see
and be seen in.

Tuxedo dark,
this night,
sewn together with
aurora borealis thoughts
and immediate intentions,
and given the finger feel
of satin sheets
or cotton briefs
simultaneously,
all caught after sundown
on the rinse cycle
of our warming machine
wired without
ground fault interruption.

That night, this night
a cover, blanket-like
and stitched together
with star scatter
from way above.

A night tapestry,
touched with exotic silk
or maybe alpaca wool,
or even bootlegged nylon
captured on booted legs,

touched with an erotic weave
over the beautiful heave
of your Angora sweater.

Now, and in one
dusk to dawn moment,
a shimmering nightshirt,
a horse blanket,
a madras military mat
for waiting out
the pending invasion.

This night
a field blanket,
a heart made wind break,
hand made for warmth's sake
and color combination
in a black and white world,
and woven with slow
carefree intimacy...
by just you
and only me.

LAKE POWELL, UTAH

Awesome rocked,
cliff power.
Unadulterated,
non-populated
Powell.

Green watered,
keen walled,
razored rocks.
A stripped clean stone base.
A rockscape.
An American Stonehenge.

The stair rocks,
are stare rocks.
The stone halls
and jut walls,
under big star ceilings,
but projectiles in miles
of rugged soul review.

Powell,
winding emerald
and jade
through rock thrusts,
cathedral canyons
and hiding coves,
so caved, carved
and mystical....
winding and calling,
though not to be dashed
upon those alluring rocks,
but only stopped and splashed
by shimmering Southwestern sun,
a real siren song
within America's Greek mythology.

Layered stone,
in caramel shades,
with ledges stacked
so incredibly high.

A sunscape.
A moonscape.
A true escape,
hinged underneath
a desert paint sky.

A river runned,
a lake dammed...
and rammed
through a canyon
so mapped
by water, wind
and time.

Powell,
winding fluid and cool,
so wrapped
and reaching
that lake...
the rocks
those canyons...
the cliffs
a languid layered
land of the gods !!!

SUMMER START

As the full clouds clear
and long rain ceases falling,
as the sun emerges
brilliant and hot,
a new season is calling
and Spring is forgot.

As the azure sky
splashes and dashes
with sunlight,
a grasshopper jumps,
a hummingbird darts,
days grow longer
with stars in the night
and Summer starts.

As a flaming sun dies,
the nightly cricket symphony
begins anew,
the stars in your eyes
the Summer magic
a reflection of you.

As we walk through
a field of wildflowers,
so beautiful
a Summer love,
Summer nights
and golden hours...

MACHO MARRIAGE, INC.

From the start...
she, was to be for him
but a proud possession,
shown off to the world,
only at appropriate times
and always
with an invisible tether line
attached to his steel meshed hand.

He, always looking,
always pulling and training.
She, flying only
in a well defined sky circle.

He, like a cruel falconer
in control
of a god beautiful bird.

He, like a master puppeteer,
with those invisible wire strings,
controlling her every movement,
her every moment.

Controlling,
not just with the manipulative dancing
of his stringed fingers,
but also with the tone of his voice,
a look, a few spoken words,
his mere marriage presence.

And over time...
he ran their marriage
like a corporation.

He, as chairman of the board.
She, as president.
He, developing, setting
and dictating policy.

She, faithfully executing
and implementing
the policy, the program.

He, the distant contact,
the aloof actor,
the silent final word,
a given.

She, the day-to-day manager,
the worker,
responsible for the operation
of the whole company.

The director and the doer.

Their bedroom,
like a boardroom,
all business,
no pleasure,
a managed agenda routine.

He, the chairman,
keeping the invisible reins tight,
and, thinking nothing
of the immediate release
of a trained, groomed
and superior subordinate,
who he had invested
so much,
yet so little in.

CHICAGO HIGHWAY APPROACH

And there,
at the highway's end
the City suddenly appears...
on and in my mind
for such a long, long time...

Now looming and rising
in the rain marred distance depth,
its jagged bold straight-line skyline,
rising up and ripping across
the muted rooted prairie horizon,
like an architectural mountain range,
with peaks and valleys
that constantly evolves and changes
in the minds and deeds
of city planners,
designers and engineers,
bankers, builders
and dreamers.

Driving on,
approaching closer and closer,
the City out there,
like a desert dessert mirage
giant eye candy
flashing distant,
glassy and glossy
through the slashing rain.

The City, that City
alluring and shimmering
like a powerful, mystical woman,
shining incandescent
through the cracked
laminated windshield
of my old red car.

Driving on,
faster and faster,
balding radial tires
hydroplaning on
the slick sly road surface,
giant raindrops
wind crawling up
the long waxed hood,
trunk tail slipping and sliding
with accelerated acceleration,
getting closer
to that steel glass welted forest, there
straddling the lake line
and piercing my prairie night.

Driving on and on
in my mindscape
between the white lines
to that cityscape,
locked in my view shed
out there pulsing
like white blips
on a night radar screen.

Driving on and on,
and getting closer
eyes laser focused ahead,
on that approaching, alluring
majestic metropolis...

Sweet Home Chicago !!!

ASH PIT SKIES

Sun gone, blue past tense.
Stacked slate stone skies now.

Horizon rising
in arch arc frame,
soldered together
with broken filament stars.

A cold ceiling roofing this
a different day,
holding earth still,
blotting and clotting
the verdant sun-sharpened colors
into layered shades of gray.

Moon mood think shift,
a silent introspect,
of stoked stone skies
slowly turning charcoal,
a giant ash pit
turned upside down…
to make me stop and think.

John V. LaMotte, Jr.

THE SHOPSTER

She is a confessed shopaholic.
A shopasauraus,
that has avoided extinction
due to the
endless proliferation
of so many stores
spread, without plan
across the land.

A small shop,
boutiques,
department stores,
an off-price outlet,
those ubiquitous
strip shopping centers,
a regional mall (heaven on earth),
Downtown,
Main Street,
Rodeo Drive,
The Magnificent Mile,
Wal-Mart,
K-Mart,
a garage sale,
and even a flea market,
keep the species alive,
to walk
and to drive,
to browse
and to shop...
and to thrive.

She is in to "power shopping",
and she is the best.

A renowned
and resourceful
retail runner,
with an appetite
so easily whetted
by so many sales
and signs.
A Saturday saler,
a merchant's marine,
battling the bargain sharks
not on beaches,
but in basements,
fighting false buyers,
those window waltzers,
not on seas
but along sidewalks.

She is an aroused
apparel trooper,
storming stores
and commanding clerks,
armed with cash,
checks and cards...
and dangerous.
Limited only by
imagination,
store hours,
and credit limits.

"Shop 'till you drop"
is her creed, as
"God put her on earth to shop",
to feed that need
to touch all the goods
and compare,
to see all the stuff
and stare,
to look,

to shop, to shop
and to shop some more,
and yes,
to finally put out
that raging, burning purse fire
and consummate
that ever so passionate
purchase desire !!!

Dedicated to my favorite shopper.

SHADOW LANDS

Shadow lands,
with shadows
that linger long along
the garage-walled alley canyons
and urban street fields
that some 60's journalist
or media mouth
once called the asphalt jungle
or was it the concrete jungle ???

Those shadows,
there in the perpetual sewer mist,
give soft delineation
to the hard, fast and real,
providing a semi-night cover,
like a brief pain killer
on short time release,
over a rough hewn day
and all that day's daily
physical imperfections,
unaccounted for
population projections,
human rejections, social outcasts
and modern day social outlaws.

That warm and fuzzy painkiller,
wearing off after 8 hours
of shadow or dark
or whichever leaves the scene
of the crime and grime first.

Can the shadow lands
be the place,
that false face place,
thought of as an

urban underground utopia
a constant cool euphoria
not for socio-economists
or political scientists,
but for a few socio-paths
and the numerous
former everyday people ???

Are they, these lands,
where mostly the lost and lonely live,
and mainly hide,
partially within the warted side
of that damn everyday,
where sun is fine
for others, somewhere
behind Foster Grants
and properly based tans,
but much too bright
and illuminatory
for those few
that foster city grants
to free base hardened snow,
and for those mostly
just lost and lonely ???

That sun light light,
a much too much bright highlight
for that which lurks, jerks,
stalks and lingers
and maybe even festers
throughout the city night,
sight unseen
and almost temporarily
or momentarily forgotten
until maybe it's too late...
A place where life cycles
lie to outsiders about the city,
a place where life

needs some light
yet, a place appreciated
for the gauze and effect
of the shadows
thrown softly around buildings
and over acne streets,
pockmarked and pitted
with political potholes,
and hidden under
broken street lamps,
pop exploded long ago
by drive-by shooters
in fluorescent Caddies
or low rider Chevys,
doing target practice
previous and prior
to their next victim,
usually the one
innocently pushing
the baby carriage
along the heaved,
cracked sidewalks.

In early evening those shadows,
get placed at random
and on purpose
here and there,
to airbrush the city's lines,
cracks and blemishes,
hiding the things
suburbanites,
conventioneers,
touristos and CEO's
are not supposed to see.

Shadows arranged to soften
the lost, the hurting,
the strange, manged and deranged,

John V. LaMotte, Jr.

like a giant monochromatic chameleon,
adjusted for slack
and soft shade intensity
but lacking brilliant hues
that may confuse their purpose…

Shadows out there,
that can diffuse so quickly
and be rearranged so efficiently
for photo opportunities
for politicians,
standing so pseudo-concerned
in front of and next to
the textured, tortured lands,
while those there,
living in those lands,
scurry like mice
with the real rats,
to seek deeper, darker
more healing shadows,
that lay even more languid and long
across the urban combat zone,
down in places
which provide photo-missed opportunities
for those who shuffle, shake and suffer,
in our stinking, screening shadow lands.

INDIGO LIES

Tell me more those indigo lies,
with minimal ties to fact
or any real database.

But they sound good
those lies, even
if they aren't so clear.

And they look good too,
especially when I'm not listening
and even if they block the view
of some rambling rainbow
I saw out on a ram ranch
along Route 66, someday ago.

Indigo lies, a falsified image...
yet, at least
a somewhat believable view
of you, and
a moment's feel good response,
as quick relief and release,
from the constant eyestrain
of the usual vixen quest.

Not even translucent
those lies,
to let a little light through.
A no clear view,
yet voluntarily I'll believe them
if it turns you on,
but, I'll turn them off
when I turn off this
one-way highway
we sometimes travel on
for fun or to just get from
Point A to Point B.

John V. LaMotte, Jr.

Someday ago,
your indigo show...
had no ray of shine
but at least
a sense of cool
and a sensation of hot
now and then.

Tell me more
those indigo lies.
I'll listen once again,
and maybe believe them
someday ago,
during a called time-out
from my vision mission
and the intermission
of your on-going indigo show.

BOLD BIRDS

Bold winter birds,
real or imaginary,
who dare to stay
and play throughout
the whipping wind season.

Bold cold birds,
who prance and dance
above the ice mist,
that rises cold cauldron like
from the hardened
glass gone lake below.

Bold brash birds
real or imaginary,
who prance
and dance
and soar
high up in
the swirling sky snows.

These birds,
those birds
their distant songs
pierce the deep set cold,
telling us
that life goes on,
even within the seemingly
forever frozen silence
of a particularly bad, bad winter.

THE SOW'S PURSE

The sow's ear,
an asymmetrical shape.

Thick.
And tough.
And tan resistant,
that sow's ear.

Yet,
flexible,
pliable
and seemingly
so viable.

Semi-smooth curved.
And quasi-haired
sparsely,
like an old wire brush....
missing the vast majority
of its bristles.

The sow's ear,
a different pork perspective,
down on the farm
or occasionally
there at the county fair.

So much more interesting.
So much more intriguing,
than a boring silk purse
hanging in pseudo-hog heaven,
along the chrome rails
at Bloomingdale's.

INDUSTRIAL ROMANCE

She had entered
and exited
an industrial romance.
Thriving, yet after all,
just surviving,
torn up inside
for reasons known,
yet never quite understood.

A once wonderful romance,
that held such early promise,
such spontaneous excitement,
such tingling sensuality
and the steady feeling
of powerful growth.

Yet, the promise and the hope
were going down
a one-way factory street.
A street with no stop signs
or other necessary and cautionary
"pause and reflect" traffic signals.

She, finally realizing the street
was not a straight line to infinity,
but was the dread dead end.

And when that realization arrived,
factory cold and smokestack gray,
acid rain began to form and fall
in her beautiful blue eye sky.
A bittersweet misting, a mixing
of clear fresh feelings
with the sulfuric emissions
of an obsolete industrial romance,

spewing grotesquely
in the toxic haste
of a shrinking, dying
love market.

THE CARPET REMNANT

The carpet remnant,
often crooked cut
and trapezoidal,
instead of a square,
or more like
a slightly leaning parallelogram
than even a precise rectangle,
and ragged a bit
at some or all its edges,
those few back strands
straying, fraying
and sometimes
even showing.

The carpet remnant
in flat floored use,
often refusing to stay put
and sliding,
and sometimes
tripping up
even the most athletic
of intellectual rug dancers.

The remnant,
so lacking in weight
due to its decreased mass
and being last
at the end of the big roll,
a little cousin
of that attractive area rug
so visible down the hall.
That loose
and shifting remnant,
often cut,
often kicked

even cursed,
and so alone.

The carpet remnant,
new, slightly odd shaped
and mostly unwanted,
yet, covering floor portions
with semi-dignity,
but, not quite the same way
as the rambling luxurious grandeur
of their raked,
shampooed, piled
and sometimes
scented mainlines.

The carpet remnant,
always being stepped on,
not with silk stockings
or clean leather under soles,
but often disgustingly wiped on
by wet and muddied boots,
appreciated only
for their scrap
of floor coverage
in those momentary times
of dirty shoe stress mess.

The remnant,
companion to few, except
the usual starving collegiate
or other poor dwellers
needing maximum coverage
with minimum bucks,
and/or those just needing
little woolly colors
on bored wood floors.

The remnant,

the savior
of traveling carpet salesmen,
the ones who just survive,
fighting direct catalog
and showroom orders.
Those salesmen,
hauling remnants
in car trunks,
who never have enough
samples or colors
or fibers or shag depths,
but usually just enough pieces
for the customer to rub.

That lonely remnant,
whose only real friend
may just be those salesmen,
or of course
good old Rover,
a constant companion
in more ways than one,
who often snores nearby
or directly above
so blissfully.

Rover,
sometimes laying
there on top,
his legs twitching
after imaginary Fifis,
while his fleas
drop down
to practice
their circus act,
in the flattened nap
of the lonely fibered
carpet remnant...

ROCKET MEN – WONDER WOMEN

London looks. Tokyo vents.
Somewhere volcanic ash
is forming under the surface
as opportunity knocks
and desire rocks.

Read demons
in singing-family houses
or in angular suites,
biting pseudo-sugar sweets
during $100 cab rides
in Beemers and designer Jeeps,
those little bullet trains,
French or Japanese,
which can pass
so much so fast,
and go somewhere
quicker, anywhere
but maybe are going nowhere.

Under high-tension lines
are high-tension lives,
living above the fray and the fury
or so they think,
like false smile frogs
sitting squat and apparently content,
on rusting lily pads afloat on PCB pools
someone once called water.

Those lives,
so near potential hairline stress fracture,
and wired with those fraying wires,
that power so many connections,
so fragile and close to the edge,
and so near that dangerous

incidental spark
that causes bad fire.

Rocket men
and wonder women,
percolating all day
like dark, pungent caffeine
in the morning rush hours,
and after hours
like fine chardonnay
escaping barrel bottom,
yet rising too fast to the top.

Those slippery skinned
daily divers, they
in IBM blue rubber skinned suits,
getting the bends
while desperately
trying to justify
the means
to their ends.

SKY PAINTER

Sky painter…on infinity canvas,
making jet stream, flak fire pieces
come so alive
on my still, yet now moving
pictured palette,
stroking with such vivid shades
and hues
and intensity
with so much promise,
movement and intention.

An in-fill density
with color runs
along color bands,
and brush streaks
expanding way past my self-imposed
silhouetted view corridor,
past the rooted earth
so easy and explored,
and into the hoped for realm
above and beyond...

Sky Paris, London,
Rome, Rio,
a small town,
downtown,
that top of the good hill...

Somewhere now,
the canvas fills
under a fireworks display
sketched without frame
but with constant crescendo,
there in a potentially long-term sky,
above shimmering ponds
that could turn golden.

Finally, a sense of civilization
emanating so from the formless
watercolor body stains
running together behind the clouds...

Passion Picassa...light up my sky !!!

THE DRUG CZARS

Only the good die young
so they say and sing,
but so too do the bad.

Good people, bad people,
both getting a crack
at crack
in a cracked
crack house.

That house,
the one down the block,
with the paper covered windows
and no solar gain,
that ominous place
with tall thistle weeds,
splintered signal stairs
and the tough door...
and the large cars
and little bicycles
parked often
in front and back.

An old house...
for the young to die good,
from the shaking, flaking spoons
of the also dying bad.

The cracked house
of the drug czars,
a fast mood operation,
with convenient service
and even quicker
drive-through.

A cracked house,
for getting jacked up, inside
before getting cracked up, outside
behind the wheel of a slick car
with illusion chrome.

The drug czars,
eventually cracking up
behind the eyes,
where the gray matter
has long been wrong
and cracked into so many pieces,
a former genetic puzzle
that will never
go back together again.

These czars,
almost like urban rulers.
Self-inflated big people
with little brain waves
and no soul train.
Born or raised killers,
ruling the 'hood
from a cracked
crack house.

A hood palace,
where the suppliers
and the liars
are framed outside
by peeling boards...
and framed inside
by razored lines on
see-me glass.

The czars,
nothing but lice lords,
hiding in a cracked

crack house.
A house containing
crazed crack dogs,
the ones with
the crusting nostrils
and the wilding eyes,
so blood red
they leave vapor trails
in the smoky chemicalled air.

The czars
and the crack dogs,
inhuman, yet
non-mammal canines...
low lives,
somewhere beneath
the animal chain and rocks,
with a low life expectancy
as they live only a high life
and a dangerous life... at best
these czars,
taking young bicycled lives
at worst.
Drug czars
in cars...
and in cracked
crack houses,
preying on infected
or neglected brains
for a quick buck joy fix,
so the easily led can escape
from someone else's
too real world,
and/or for descent
into their much desired
earth hell,
that hell situation,
seen too often now

on the evening news,
whereby glazed,
crazed crack dogs
in $130 athletic shoes,
run and rule the streets,
free to kill at will for fun
so terribly fueled
by the fire snow
of the deadly urban drug czars.

A PRAIRIE SERMON

On tall grass plains
above thick thorn thickets
and directly under
a setting, sitting sun,
a raw sweeping wind
from whole day through,
gathers now the shadows
lingering out behind
the sparse hickory clusters
past the last plow row
there in the buck bush bottom.

A churchman's voice
in steady sermon sequence,
rings out... strong and clear
within the candled dusk
and between the high caliber bullets
traveling long and low
through that bog wind.

Those aimed city bullets,
pierce the clean country air
like the churchman's plea...
yet, eventually lose velocity
and intention,
and lodge miles away
down in the dark prairie loam...
target missed.

Those bullets,
in their trailing trajectory,
part the reaching corn,
and burrow deep thin holes
for new seeds to grow
a soulful supper feeding.

The churchman's voice
in inspiration, raised...
calls upon the plainsman's choice
to toil long and hard
under the trying, drying sun,
to see for miles and miles,
to sometimes stand so alone
and to bring life...
to the bulleted ground holes.

LAKE ARROWHEAD, CALIFORNIA

March 2010

They look out across
a magical, majestic
mountain range
and at her
liquid lanquid
love lake
so far down below,
and history is made…
with a question,
an answer,
a pine cone and
the promise of diamonds
and a life filled with so much love…

POETRY

Hard line illustration,
soft sketched imagination.

Inspired red blood
and the quiet passion
that flows invisibly
yet so intensely through it.

A blend of reality
and fantasy.
A solid concrete floor
beneath transparent
imagery ceilings,
structurally connected
with fact and fiction
or faction.

Original, yet allegorical.
Mini-stories... with a twist.

Music-less word scores
and mesmerizing mental images,
seeking immediate release
or long-term escape,
which ever comes first.

Mind photos,
burned forever
in black and white
and in color
on the whitest
of non-film paper
and in the bluest corners
of daydreams.

Word sculptures,
shaped by rapid transit impulses
and/or deep organic thoughts
that only a few, if any
may comprehend.

Straightforward knowledge
and carefully crafted metaphors,
yet, powerful exploding
thought fragments,
valued both for idle inspiration
or someday synergy.

Loose brain banter
from deep in gray matter
or close to the surface
heart pulses
and even introspective
soul searches
with sensitivity sparks.

Vision taps
and psychic tips.
Logic loops,
amidst syntax symmetry.
An unholy word order
within rigid rack rhetoric.

A looking back.
A seeking forward.
The constant searching,
on a continuum
of retrospection
and projection,
in rear view mirrors
and crystal balls,
for people and places past,
for what seems now,
for pre-game predictions.

But all,
maybe just ink lines
running in place
like wayward electricity
on flat transmission pages.

All in all,
the make-believe work products
of a semi-skilled wordsmith
stopping...
to see the forest
for the trees.

ABOUT THE AUTHOR

Born and raised in Chicago and its suburbs, John LaMotte has been writing poetry since his childhood. Inspired by city and country as well as family and friends, his clear poetry style evokes laughter, reflection and some times pain.

John is a professional city planner with extensive experience in land use planning, urban design and community development. He has been a senior member of two international design firms and the former Chicago Department of Economic Development. In 1993 he co-founded The Lakota Group, a widely recognized consulting firm based in Chicago that provides services in Planning, Urban Design, Landscape Architecture, Historic Preservation and Community Relations.

He is also a trained mediator and has been actively involved in the leadership of several professional and civic groups, including the Metropolitan Planning Council, American Planning Association, El Valor Corporation and Chicago Public Art Group. He has been a speaker, panelist and facilitator at numerous planning and development conferences, workshops and seminars throughout his career.

John has a Masters of Urban & Regional Planning from University of Wisconsin-Madison and a Bachelors in Geography-Urban Planning from University of Utah.

John has worked with thousands of people across the country to plan and change the future of their cities and villages. He has facilitated hundreds of town hall meetings, community workshops, focus groups and interviews. He brings vision, compassion, communication skills, a robust sense of humor and "rhinoceros skin" to his daily work and to his poetry...